finish this sentence

finish
this
sentence

poetry

leslie roach

MAWEN**Z**I
HOUSE

We acknowledge the support of the Canada Council for the Arts for our publishing program. We also acknowledge support from the Government of Ontario through the Ontario Arts Council, and the support of the Government of Canada through the Canada Book Fund.

Cover design by Sabrina Pignataro

Cover photo: Pattadis Walarput / Abstract black dust explosion stock photo / iStockphoto

Author photo credit: Kayla Straker-Trotman

Title: Finish this sentence : poetry / Leslie Roach.

Names: Roach, Leslie, 1976- author.

Identifiers: Canadiana (print) 20200326287 | Canadiana (ebook) 20200326414 | ISBN 9781774150269

(softcover) | ISBN 9781774150276 (EPUB) | ISBN 9781774150283 (PDF)

Subjects: LCSH: Racism—Poetry.

Classification: LCC PS8635.O1216 F56 2020 | DDC C811/.6—dc23

Printed and bound in Canada by Coach House Printing

Mawenzi House Publishers Ltd.
39 Woburn Avenue (B)
Toronto, Ontario M5M 1K5
Canada

www.mawenzihouse.com

Contents

Foreword

Racism is society's plague, affecting countless people in myriad ways every day. Unfortunately, we live in a world where oppression takes root. As for me, racism affected my mental sanity from a very young age. It provoked trauma, which made me feel constantly under siege—you never know when you will be attacked again. A few years ago, I realized that I needed to heal. My objective with this work was to call out racism and to illustrate its effects on the psyche. As this work weaves through the anger and anxiety provoked by racism, it points to the ultimate realization, which is that I am neither the conditioning nor the incessant chatter that racism provoked. Rather, I am powerful and able to arrest those harmful thoughts. Awakening to these truths has helped me to heal. I hope this work will be beneficial to others as well.

My Black Man, Maybe You Don't Know

But I try to
Spare you
Going into
Harm's
Way
By doing
As many
Of the
Groceries
For us
As I can.
Black women
Aren't as
Much a threat as
A Black man. They
Can always rape
Me, but they
Can kill
You.
No wonder
Black mothers,
Especially of
Boys,
Go crazy

Being Black

When you're Black
you feel all
eyes on
you.

And they
are.

It's not
just
you.

They
are!

See Title Below

The fortitude of Black people, to encounter this world and not go mad. To chronically tone down the experience. The hardship, enduring madness, being mad and still having to survive and actually thriving at times and then brought back down to take your place, to be in that place of meekness, bleakness (You're fierce).
But still scared. What if tomorrow I can't do it anymore. What if tomorrow I can't get up anymore. What if the mobs do finally get me.
Know those demons are there. Know that they are there but let them walk alongside you, don't let them get in your way.

Toning it down & reconciling

Venture There

To be present. Anywhere. To venture there where you feel like you can't. Like you're not welcome. Like you can't or shouldn't be there. That feeling is one I feel a lot. I need to get over that. To purify, petrify those thoughts from my mind. And I've found a way. To be in place everywhere. The conditioning of this mind was such that you were better seen than heard. That you be still. That you not do or say anything out of place. That you be stuck. Complacent. So agreeing that you get lost. So lost.

You must go there.

Fate Talks to Faith

But they seem to be
enjoying this
samsara,
they are
thriving,
aren't they?

But what about us—
are we the lucky, morally
fit ones that get
tortured
so that
we get
to transcend?

Afros Don't Yield

The last thing I
want to
do
is touch this
Afro.

Taming it,
getting it to
yield
without
nuff
grease
is
near
impossible.

Leaves arms
tired.

Fear Makes You Hate, Can I Really Ever Trust You?

I'm scared that the zombies come out of the woodworks,
That it's a real living dead type thing and
the ghost faces
gather like zombies in
horror movies and try to get us.

Advice to a reluctant soul looking for approval on the way forward, but already knows the way, it makes you want to do

It makes you want to do.
And that in the end is what it's about.

Serial killers don't stop
to think about you, if you like
what they want to do.
They just do.
This is merely the best advice on life I've ever received.

Dream the impossible dream.

They See But Don't See You

Sometimes I can't take
the absurdity of
what is/are
social norms in
Canada.

People see but
don't see you.

People you see
every day.
Might dodge you like the
plague.

Just cause they don't
want to say
hi.

Evolutionary Processing

Realizing that people aren't where you assumed they should
be at in their evolution. Just because someone has grey
hair or black doesn't mean that they are enlightened. Far
from. What scares me the most is realizing how much pain
I inflicted on myself due to my conditioning. I knew long
ago that conditioning was a big part of it. I knew. From early
on. That something was wrong. Profoundly wrong with
accepting the other as better and constantly having to gesture
or not for them. How on the one hand can they expect you to
be silent and then also to gesture for them and be the clown.
The clown who knows their place. Who is silent. Who is
reserved. That I don't understand. Finding one's place can be
difficult.

I'm talking to you of whom the world is not worthy.
They'll flip the script on you.
Be wary.

Go, I implore you.
Go. Find that place which is
home.

Let the assaults come as they may.
And do what is necessary at the time.

I Promise You

One day
we'll
revolt.

Again.

I promise you.

Provincial Home Town Coming

Back to my home town coming to the realization that my home city is no place for me despite all that our parents did to make it so. It's a city on the decline for me—those not "de souche" are increasingly pushed to the sidelines. Born and raised there. Parents immigrated in the 1960s but you are forever foreign in your own land. They see you and judge. It's provincial.

I was on the cusp of sovereignty as I lived abroad and thought "on est bien chez nous". I celebrated St. Jean abroad. But upon return to my promised land, with the wrong name and shade, I couldn't find work; was told that I now lacked Canadian experience, having worked for the United Nations for too long. I felt the margins within the margins. Relegated to applying to firms west of the main to accommodate my tongue and face, and then seeing the slim pickings, even the insular Anglo bastions (who was I kidding) could provide reprieve. Not wanting to be a customer service agent, I left. Maybe Ottawa would be better.

Soul Occupied

I feared Tweeting,
or Liking on Twitter
for fear of some
future employer not liking
it. Clearly I shouldn't
worry about some
non-entity
who wouldn't hire
me anyways.
That's where they
are getting it wrong.
You took, are taking,
keep taking away
the little hope we
had. We could maybe
have survived on little
hope, but no
hope . . .

Well, it ushers an end.

Not Me

They'll say it wasn't me.
It wasn't me
who ignored
that guy
who came into
our workplace
and greeted everyone
every day until
he noticed that
no one else really
bothered.
He got tired.
He heard them
laughing, huddled
in groups together,
he was
quite alone.

He looked to
get
back.

Unsure

Some days I feel
like eradicating
it.

That's how
out of
place
I feel.

The idea
of community is
almost always
exclusive.

So not
you.

The politics of course,
are ego
centric.

But what's
good
for me
is good
for you &
vice
versa.

Lost Innocence

Imagine if the kids knew that their fate was in our hands.

Untitled

When the law gives
you less
protection than
another category
of person,
you have the
Divine right
to claim
the protection
of God.

They Say I Have TMJ

They uncovered
something wrong
with my mouth

They said
I clench
my teeth
so

I lack overbite

So the stress
in my mouth
is constant

It rings a bell

It's true:
I don't know
how to place
my mouth

It's never comfortable

I now have TMJ

Ironic to find
out now

That I don't have
A problem

With my mouth

My Family's Poetry

We laughed. I love
my family. So
grateful, we have known such laughter.

That I can't control
myself laughter. That
love. I'd do anything
for you laughter.

We are good
Oh so good.
But that pain of racism
permeated everything
for us.

It is our reality.
I don't know how
it affected the
others, I can't
say, we don't talk about
it much, but as for
me, it makes me
constantly afraid.

But lately the fear
is morphing into
its opposite and
I'm so happy.

It's the I don't
give a f***
kind of happy,
It's you're s***

happy.
Not *you* but that too.
It's you other person: you are s*** and I
don't give a f***.
Get out of my way
kind of f***.
I don't care if
you run me over kind of
f***.

Didn't every noble
cause, cause spark—
some Noble Prize?

My eye is on the Prize.
Real revolution is still due.
Look at the unfairness that
permeates the
world over.
This place is just
less corrupt
than others and
I should thank God for that
And shut
up, no.
My life has
been made
hell due
to racism.
The dialogue
that never
stops within
due to how
you've
excluded me.

Made into
dirty when
I'm so f******
Clean.

F*** you.
My man says all
man for himself:
we are not saints.
We do all
things that
benefit us.
All of us.
So what—
leave it
as a
dog eat
dog
world?

I don't know.

Shattered

I would be
lying if
I said
this
journey
was
not
born
of
racism.

I remember
a time
when
I
saw no
differences
among
people.

I loved
everyone
and had
empathy
for
all.

I started
to feel hate
in
grade 1
because
I was

called
nigger
a
lot.

I remember
trying to
carve the
word
"Black"
in my
hands
one day
standing
near the
water fountains
at school.

It hurt.

I remember
breaking the
window
in my
parents'
bedroom
in
grade 2 or 3.

That's because
I was
knocking
on it so
hard.

Some girls

were playing together
in the road.
They were so
free.

I was knocking
on the
window
crying
wishing
it
was
me.

The window
broke.

I didn't
really
care.

I made
something
up.

I said
a rock
hit the
window
and it
broke.

When the repair
men
came,
they told
my

parents
that it
looked
like it
came from
the inside
because of
the way
the glass
had
shattered.

My parents
didn't believe
them.

Thankfully,
they were
always on
my
side.

I Never Knocked

I've wondered why
I never
knocked when
I
was left
out
in the
dark hallway.

It was
dark
in that building
and I was
scared.

And yet I never
knocked
to the
voices inside
at the party.

To let me
in.

I just cried.

Get Out

They
want you
uncomfortable.

If you relax
in their
midst
you're
marked
for
target.

It might
let them on
to something
so I hold
my head
down.

But I never was comfortable ever, anywhere,
never really comfortable,
that's what racism does
anyway.

But lately
I've
been seeing
the
real truth.

It started
with James
Baldwin, Maya

Angelou, Audre
Lorde.
They spoke to me.
When comfort seemed even more
elusive.

Said what I
knew but hadn't
dared think.
It was
worse than I thought.

It made me
angry.
Rightfully angry.
I didn't dare
bow my
head again.

Man it's vile.

From that anger vocalized.
I needed a master.
I found Mooji.
Spirituality calling louder
than ever.

I found
release in the
infinite.

And see ever more
what
power I
have.

What incredible

power of
transcendence.

I have made
It. My conditioning
doesn't exist
if I don't
buy into
It.

I think I'm
out of these
chains.
And yet
too many
a
brother
in chains
for nothing
or
dead.

It goes in
circles and
loops.

I want out
of this Samsara.

Oh

Oh, What a glorious
place
to be
on top
of the dregs of
humanity.
Shit hard
but imagine how
real
hard it would
be if
you were
one of them.

The Poor Majority

Why couldn't a poor person be president or prime minister?
But he already is.
I mean why couldn't a real poor person be president or prime
minster?
We are a minority.
No we are a majority.
Collectively.

I Am Not One Minority

I am not One
Get Over the Minority Mentality

They want you where
they want you

That's why they try to divide
That's why they call us
"minorities"
or preferably,
"a minority"
By yourself.

Dividing and
Conquering.
. . .

So they deal with you as
a "minority".
Some collectivities—
they help
each other
out.

Let Me Be

That's the problem
with the world.

So just do this:

I make room for
you to pass by.

Give me room
to pass by.

Stand clear of
my potential.

And I stand
clear of yours.

Let me Be.

And I'll let you
Be too.

Billionaire Mentality

This 21st century has brought more fear. You'd think
we would have figured it out by now. You'd think that
enlightenment would have caught up. That people would
have gotten over this shit. Instead it's gotten worst. They
knew something that we didn't. That the dregs of society are
still rampant. They are at large. Among us. You don't know.
You don't know if your neighbour plans to eat you. You don't
know. And that's where they stand among us. They are the
people eaters. The people haters. They are at the table. Why
are we even debating this? That is what's scary about this.
That people don't see. It's sad. I don't even know how we
continue. But we do. We try. We get on with it. We take the
bull by the horns and dance with the devil. We have to. They
left us no choice. Unless we rally, there is nothing we can do.
And they are experts at dividing and conquering.

An Appraisal

The
last thing I need is
praise.

From the likes
of you.

Sunscreen at the Work BBQ

At the summer
BBQ
She asked me
if I wanted
sunscreen
in case I
didn't want
to get too
Black.

I told her
no, I have
no problem
with getting
Blacker.

She said oh,
because she
had a
friend who
didn't want
to get
too Black.

Shame that!
Not enough
is said about
that.

Yes, you feel
the pressure

to be the
least
Black
possible, in
all ways.

Rally On

We tasted hope.
With Obama.

I never thought
I could see
this in my
lifetime.

Imagine those
who had
lived through
the movement.

Had bet years
earlier that
the first
would have
been
female.

And not
Black!

On the Line

Ok. This is what
we're dealing with.
This is why I write.
To know
on the line
That I am not
mad.
Seeing it on the line
somehow helps me
to know
better.

Don't Stand By

Those who have
the power to
mobilize will
inherit the earth.

Why Racism Is Dangerous, Even for You

It strips you
of your humanity.

And we could act
accordingly.

Cast Away

Feeling like a
cast away
in plain
sight
has been
my plight.

A Real Number

That's the kind of
number

it
plays on you.

It put hounds on you/
in you.

Right of Way

A real number.

Keeps us from crossing
at intersections—
lest we be
run over.

We've never had the
right
of way.

Before They Got Hold of You

Being
is the only
way out
of this misery
inflicted
and you believing.

See it
for what
It is.

And return to
your natural
state.

The state
before they
got hold of
you and
told you
everything
about you
was
wrong.

See It for What It Is

Recognize the
delusion

Why defend
the
illusion

Only be your
Self.

And carry on.

No Reason

It is for you
I do this.

For you, that
little girl
made into a
demon for
no reason.

Weather

The umbrella allows
my invisibility—
a cloak to navigate
this world a while
in obscurity.

A lot of us
folk love the
rain for
this reason.

Hoods offer the
same protection
but can
backfire.
RIP Trayvon Martin.

Disarming

I was armed by the
harm done, the
armour suited me
well.

But since I was
suited by
you,

I want no
part in
that arm.

My Rebellion

I'm simply letting go.
Of any
label
meant to be
attached
to me.

Refusing
to let anyone
define my humanity.

Understanding

Understanding why this Black Woman was feeling so
dejected and rejected and visible and yet invisible came from
Audre Lorde, James Baldwin, Toni Morrison, Maya Angelou,
Alice Walker, Nina Simone. You cannot deny the importance
of art. They let me know I wasn't crazy, but was going crazy
based on circumstances and giving people permission to
define my humanity.

Years ago, Toni Morrison's novel *The Bluest Eye* put me on
notice.

Manifest

As a total and
utter outcast
—you can't
take it
forever.

At some point
you break.

In breaking,
you break
with "reality."

And say
who are you
to tell
me
who
I am?

And it
spills out from
there.

Go with it.

See/feel
what your
body is
telling
you.

Stay there.

Feel that opening.

The one
that is
free of
anything.

Take that
route.

Before you
know it.

You won't
even
recognize
yourself.

Anything is
possible
from
there.

Take
that route.

Tap
into this.

The promised
land rests
just there.

. . .

But what they
want
is

to keep
you afraid—

have you see
the headlines

Black face
left & right.

Bulleted through.

Scared, right?
They want
us scared.

Who's coming
for you.

Who's around
the corner?

Who's profiling
you?

It lurks.

And hurts.

Always.

The mistake
they made is
that it can't
hurt always.

Because you
step out.

You see how
they made
you crazy.

Paranoid.
Schizophrenic.

Never safe
anywhere.

Yes, you are responding
to a real threat.

It's war that no
one declared
and
it's
against
you.

No wonder
you
go
crazy.

It's rampant.

You have
PTSD.

You can't get
ahead.

You're hungry.

Tired.

Assaulted.

It's too much & . . . then
you
step out.

You opt
out.

You say

No, thank you.

Love was never
served here.

You realize,
see, feel,
hear how
wrong it all
is.

If
you
see
what
they've
done.

How messed
up it
is.

But I
mean
clearly—
you're
no
longer

trapped.

Just
like
that.

And
that's
one
fierce
being.

That has
emerged
from
all this
shit.

Tis
Black Magic.

Embrace it all
fully. Embrace
the wrong.

See how that feels.

Living in the
present
moment
tells you all
that.

You feel that it
is apart
from you.

Like a bubble
floating away
that has
nothing to do
with you.

Never has.

See this.

You have been
excluded
from
all of this.

It's like
a circus.

A big top
with fools performing
and you
were typecast.

No thank you.

It's all very
unattractive.

It offers you
nothing nor
can it
enhance you.

I'm fine
thank you.

I'm not
going on

with this
charade—
I'm not even
there
anymore.

Exit stage left.

I'm in a different
place.

Responding to the
space the
moment affords.

It is there
that
we manifest.

Our true power.

Power

Thank you for
excluding
me so
much.

I got so
fed up

that I
found
my
way

out.

Laying Low

The thing is
they walk
by thinking
I'm not
fine.

I'm fine
laying low
like that.

They don't know
what
I
know.

This Force

This force
is
not
a
fight
though.

It is
a
refusal
to be
dominated.

It is a
protection
of
Self.

Movement Appeal

I hope this
movement
won't
lose it's
appeal
for being
based
in the
Present.

And not
being a
fight.

What power
it offers
as a result.

Inflicting

Inflicting more
and more
hurt on
the victim.

Soon
or late, the victim
can't take it
anymore.

And unbeknown
to you
and suddenly
no longer
sees himself
that way.

It creates a way.

A space has been
made.

And he is
served first
among equals.

Stop Me in My Tracks

Sometimes still
you stop
me in
my tracks
because
I
have a
natural
reflex
towards
decency.

I'll never
treat that
as weakness.

Despite how
easy it
would be
for me.

I just need
to respond
to the present—
that's
how I know
how
to respond
to you.

And move on.

No Title Needed

I have eliminated those
things which no
longer serve me.

You Want Me

You want me
quiet, complacent.

You think
me
dormant
in
your
midst.

Ironically then,
when
I'm happy
and find
things to do
with this
solitude
you've imposed
on me,
you're suspicious
of what
you
see.

Still

Still I need
To
Relax
Those
Muscles
Made
Tense
And
Jittery From all This.
It takes
Its
Toll.

Acknowledgments

My beloved James, you amaze me. You have shown me your magic. I hope to do it justice.

My beloved Kofi, you have helped me to see the power we wield.

My dear parents, you live forever more as a testimony of love, wisdom and understanding. You fueled me with belief. What more could a child hope for?

Lisa and Jamie, you have always been there for me and each other. That alone is a testimony to our upbringing.

Ren, I knew you from the start and you are my dear sister. I know you will understand the words in this book as I feel they are yours too.

Richard, we are so happy to have met you. I can't believe we got so lucky.

Cherie, Rob, Kristin, Parvati, and so many others, you are family.

To my muse, which is simply the inspiration which comes to play and pours the words onto the page leaving me complete in that moment, with a better understanding of my situation, I am humbled by you.